The publisher would like to thank Ron Ridout of Bird Studies Canada for checking the text and illustrations.

Groundwood Books / House of Anansi Press
groundwoodbooks.com

We gratefully acknowledge for their financial support of our publishing program the Canada Council for the Arts, the Ontario Arts Council and the Government of Canada.

Canada Council   Conseil des Arts
for the Arts   du Canada

ONTARIO ARTS COUNCIL
CONSEIL DES ARTS DE L'ONTARIO
an Ontario government agency
un organisme du gouvernement de l'Ontario

With the participation of the Government of Canada
Avec la participation du gouvernement du Canada | Canada

Library and Archives Canada Cataloguing in Publication
Vande Griek, Susan, author
An owl at sea / Susan Vande Griek ; illustrated by Ian Wallace.
Issued in print and electronic formats.
ISBN 978-1-77306-111-5 (hardcover). — ISBN 978-1-77306-112-2 (PDF)
1. Short-eared owl — Biography — Juvenile literature. 2. Wildlife rescue — Juvenile literature. I. Wallace, Ian, illustrator II. Title.
QL696.S83V36 2019   j598.9'70929   C2018-904235-4
C2018-904236-2

The art for this book was created in watercolor on Fabriano Artistico watercolor paper, handmade from 100% natural cotton, chlorine and acid-free. This paper has been produced in Italy since 1264 and was valued by artists such as Michelangelo and Leonardo da Vinci.
Design by Michael Solomon
Printed and bound in Malaysia

For the owl rescuers, on land and
at sea. — SVG

To Michael and Nan,
with gratitude for everything you
do that enriches my work,
and in memory of Sheila,
who offered me this evocative
story to draw. — IW

AN OWL AT SEA

SUSAN VANDE GRIEK

ART BY
IAN WALLACE

GROUNDWOOD BOOKS
HOUSE OF ANANSI PRESS
TORONTO   BERKELEY

*T*his owl,
smallish owl,
mottled brown,
round head,
belongs here,
hovering over grassy field,
floating over misty marsh,
yellow eyes sharp,
hunting a meal —
tiny vole,
little mouse —
perching over open ground,
keen ears alert
to rustle or chirp.

So what is it doing
way out here,
far, far out
over open water,
over grassless sea
where mackerel and herring,
haddock and cod
are all there is
for a bird to eat?

Wings rowing slowly,
beating long,
eyes searching for field or fencepost,
but finding none.
No place to rest,
no mouse to hear,
only the swing,
the roar
of the sea,
so gray, so near.

A weary owl,
a silent owl,
flying and flying,
mile after mile.
Until
it falls from the sky
when it suddenly spies
a spot
on the water,
a platform riding high.

Chunky legs,
tired wings
drop,
fold,
talons searching
for something to hold.
The owl goes down
hard,
fast,
grounded at last,
but on an oil rig
anchored miles offshore.

There's no grass,
no field,
no mouse,
no vole,
only hard, cold metal,
ladders and posts.

But the owl's exhausted,
closes wings and eyes.
It huddles down —
it can't go on.

And it isn't long
before
one oil rigger,
then two, then three
discover it there.
They stop.
They stare.
Then shake their heads
in disbelief.

For what is an owl
of field and tree
doing here —
here on an oil rig
moored on water,
one hundred miles out
on the heaving gray sea?

"Lost its way, for sure,"
they murmur,
they fret.
But what to do?
Can't say, "Be off.
Fly away home,"
for it's tired and weak,
and likely not knowing
what direction
it needs to go
or keep.

So, hands in gloves,
the workers move
quietly,
slowly
to pick it up,
bring it in from the wet,
find a boxed-in corner,
a blanket for a bed,
some bits of meat
to keep it fed.

Riggers stop by,
look in,
curious,
close,
and think how it's strange
that creatures of the earth,
like the owl,
like them,
should end up out here,
so far from land.

Weakened
and stressed,
the owl watches,
the owl rests.
And in a few days
another bird,
immensely big,
hovers, then lands,
sets down on the rig.

The copter's unloaded,
refueled,
soon ready to fly,
but this time carrying something more
than men and supplies.
It carries the riggers,
it carries their gear,
it carries one owl
far from home,
short-eared.

Airborne again,
but this time in flight,
the owl's wings
are closed
and held in
tight.

A ride back to land,
to where an owl belongs,
a ride back for riggers,
to families waiting on shore.

And when they arrive
there's a bird-rescue team
waiting for an owl
found at sea.

They transport the bird
to their shelter,
their aviary.

There the owl is cared for,
examined and fed.
In days it becomes stronger,
lively and well,
and when it's recovered
the bird rescuers know
they can free the owl.
They can let it go.

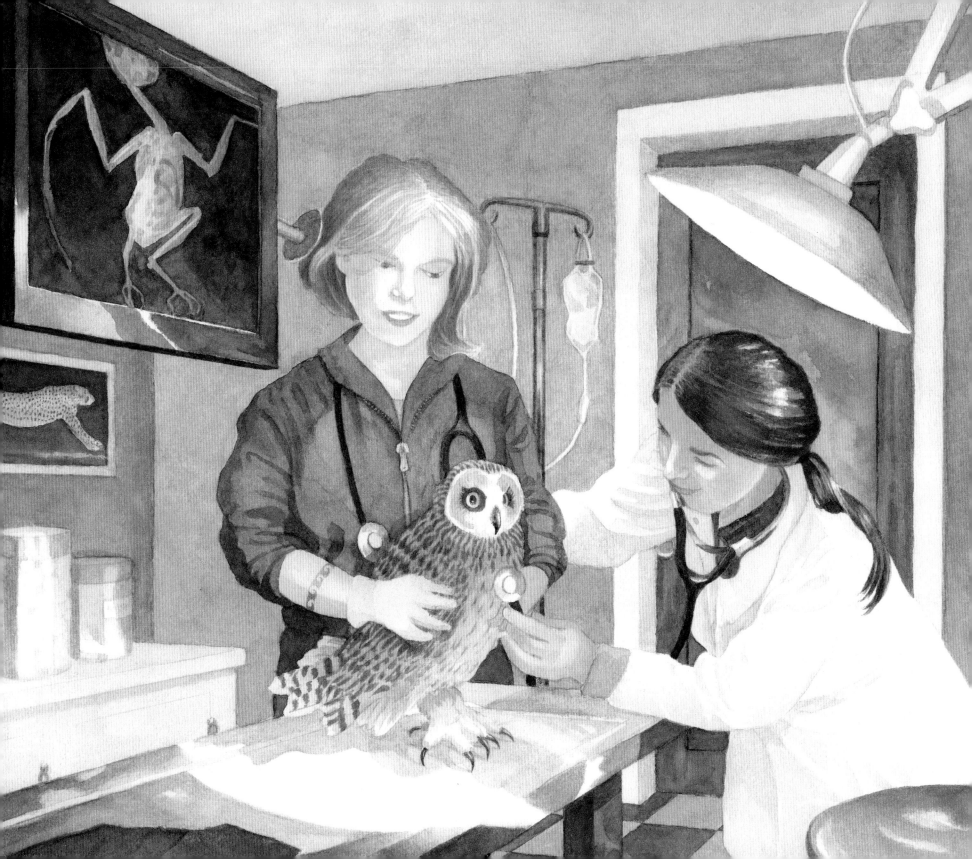

It's released over grass field,
over wide-open space.
Wings spread,
floating high
then fluttering low,
patrolling for prey,
the Short-eared Owl
is at home
to stay,
here
far, far
from the sea,
from that cold ocean spray.

The Short-eared Owl
Asio flammeus

I wrote this story after reading a newspaper report about an owl that, strangely enough, plummeted down onto an oil-drilling platform in the North Sea, off the coast of Scotland. Why did this owl of field and marsh end up on a steel structure surrounded by water, far from its normal habitat? Perhaps it became confused in stormy weather or when flying from one feeding area to another, maybe even from as far away as Scandinavia. It was taken in and cared for, first by the oil-rig workers and then by the Scottish SPCA. When the owl recovered from its ordeal at sea, it was released back into its natural habitat.

This bird was a Short-eared Owl, named for its tiny feathery ear tufts that are not truly ears at all. The Short-eared Owl feeds on mice, voles and other small mammals or birds that it hunts in fields, prairies, tundra and marshes. It flies slowly, hovering over open ground, and it is active early and late in the day, which make it easier to spot than most types of owls.

Usually a fairly solitary and quiet bird, the male may hoo when looking for a mate, and both male and female may make a barking sound when disturbed. Sometimes when courting, these owls flap their wings together, almost as if they were clapping. Nests are little more than scraped-out areas on the ground, lined with feathers and grass. Four to eight eggs are laid in the spring. About six weeks after hatching, young owls leave the nest.

Short-eared Owls are found in North and South America, as well as in Europe and Asia. Though not considered endangered, these owls may face a decline in numbers due to a loss of habitat.

SOURCES

"Owl air lifted to safety after crash-landing on North Sea oil rig." *The Independent*, October 28, 2015, https://www.independent.co.uk/news/uk/home-news/owl-air-lifted-to-safety-after-crash-landing-on-north-sea-oil-rig-a6712281.html.

"Owl airlifted twoo safety after crash landing on oil rig." *The Telegraph*, October 28, 2015, https://www.telegraph.co.uk/news/earth/wildlife/11960517/Owl-airlifted-twoo-safety-after-crash-landing-on-oil-rig.html.

FURTHER READING

Short-eared Owls
allaboutbirds.org/guide/Short-eared_Owl
owlworlds.com/short-eared-owl
onnaturemagazine.com/short-eared-owl.html

Oil Rigs
Life on an Oil Rig by Drew Nelson, Gareth Stevens, 2013